The Nature Kid's Guide to
LADYBUGS

DAVID ANDERSON

For information address LP Media Inc. Publishing,
30012 Variolite St NW, Princeton MN 55371
www.lpmedia.org

Publication Data

Ladybugs
The Nature Kid's Guide to Ladybugs — First edition.

Summary: "Learn all about Ladybugs, the Nature Kid Way"
— Provided by publisher.

ISBN: 979-8-89818-201-4

[1. Ladybugs – Non-Fiction] I. Title.

Title: The Nature Kid's Guide to Ladybugs

CONTENTS

LEAFY LANDS

There are over 5,000 species of ladybug in the world — and they come in yellow, orange, black, and even completely spotless!

Buzz! A little ladybug lands on a sunny garden leaf.

Ladybugs live in many places. You can find them in gardens, fields, and forests. They love spots with lots of plants.

These tiny bugs like warm, sunny places best. They rest on leaves and stems during the day. Some live in meadows full of wildflowers, while others live near ponds and streams.

A ladybug picks its home with care. It needs plants and food close by. Flowers, bushes, and vegetable gardens are some of their favorite spots to call home.

WORLD WIDE

Whoosh! A ladybug rides the wind across a wide green meadow.

Ladybugs live all over the world. You can find them on every continent except Antarctica. It is simply too cold there for these small bugs.

Some kinds live in hot, dry deserts. Others live in cool, wet forests.

Each part of the world has its own special types. In North America, one common kind has orange wings with black spots. No matter where you live, ladybugs are probably nearby.

In many countries, people think ladybugs bring good luck — some even make wishes on them!

TINY TOTS

FUN FACT!

Some ladybugs have stripes instead of spots — and a few have no markings at all!

Tick! A tiny ladybug crosses a penny in just a few small steps.

Ladybugs are very small. Most are about the size of a pea. They can be as tiny as a grain of rice or as big as a raisin.

Even though they are small, they are easy to see. Their bright colors pop against green leaves. You can spot one right away!

A ladybug weighs less than a paper clip. You could hold ten of them in one hand, but be gentle if you do! These little bugs are tougher than they look.

BODY BITS

A ladybug's thin wings can beat about 85 times in one single second!

Click! A yellow ladybug lifts its hard shell and spreads its wings.

A ladybug has three main body parts. It has a head, a middle part, and a back end. Six short legs help it walk and climb.

On top sits a hard, round shell called the **elytra**. This shell keeps the soft wings safe underneath. When a ladybug wants to fly, it lifts its shell and unfolds its delicate wings. The whole process takes less than one second!

A ladybug also has two short feelers on its head. These feelers help it smell, taste, and find its way around.

SENSE STUFF

A ladybug can taste with its feet just by walking on a leaf!

Sniff! A ladybug wiggles its tiny feelers and smells food nearby.

Ladybugs use their senses to explore the world. They smell and touch with their feelers, called **antennae**. These antennae pick up scents floating in the air.

Ladybug eyes are special. Each eye is made of many tiny parts — sometimes hundreds! They can see colors and light, but shapes look blurry to them.

Tiny hairs on a ladybug's body can feel the wind blow. These hairs warn them if something big is coming close. Every part of their body helps them survive.

SPOT SHOCK

Some ladybugs are black with red spots instead of red with black spots!

Flash! A bird sees a bright red ladybug and flies away fast.

Ladybugs have a secret weapon. Their bright colors warn other animals to stay away. Red, orange, and yellow all say the same thing: 'I taste bad!'

Most ladybugs have black spots on their shells. Some have just two spots. Others have seven, fourteen, or even more! The spots help scare off hungry birds and other animals.

This trick is called warning coloration. It tells predators that the ladybug would make a terrible meal. Those bright colors keep them safe day after day.

BUG BITES

DID YOU KNOW?
One ladybug can eat more than 5,000 aphids in its whole life!

Crunch! A ladybug bites into a juicy aphid on a garden branch.

Ladybugs love to eat **aphids**. Aphids are tiny, soft bugs that live on plants. A single ladybug can eat 50 aphids in one day!

But aphids are not their only food. Some ladybugs also eat mites and small insects. A few kinds even munch on plants and pollen instead.

Ladybugs are hungry little bugs. They need to eat a lot to stay strong and healthy. In a garden, one ladybug can gobble up hundreds of aphids each week.

MUNCH MODE

FUN
FACT!
Ladybugs do not have teeth —
they chew food with tiny strong
jaws called mandibles!

Chomp! A ladybug crawls down a stem and snatches a tiny aphid.

Ladybugs are great hunters. They walk along stems and leaves to find food. When they spot a bug, they grab it with their jaws and chew it up.

A ladybug does not chase its food. Instead, it walks slowly until it bumps into a meal. Then it holds the bug down and eats it bit by bit.

Ladybugs also eat soft bug eggs for extra energy. Nothing goes to waste when you are this hungry!

WATCH OUT

DID YOU KNOW?
Some ants protect aphids from ladybugs like tiny bodyguards — and even fight them off!

Swoop! A hungry bird darts down toward a little ladybug on a dandelion.

Ladybugs have many predators. Birds, spiders, and frogs all like to eat them. Even some wasps and flies hunt ladybugs.

Big insects can be a problem too. Dragonflies and praying mantises catch ladybugs in the wild. These hunters are fast and very hard to escape.

Being small can be risky. But ladybugs are tough little bugs with many tricks to stay alive. They survive in a world full of hungry predators every single day.

STAY SAFE

FUN FACT!
The yellow liquid from a ladybug's legs is actually its own blood!

Plop! A ladybug drops off a leaf and plays dead on the ground.

When a ladybug is scared, it has tricks. One trick is to drop off the leaf and fall to the ground. It tucks in its legs and plays dead until danger passes.

Ladybugs can also push out a stinky yellow liquid from their legs. This juice smells bad and tastes even worse! Most predators spit the ladybug right out.

If all else fails, a ladybug can fly away fast. It lifts off the leaf and zooms to safety in seconds. Speed is its best escape plan.

FLY FAST

DID YOU KNOW?
A ladybug can fly at speeds up to 15 miles per hour — as fast as a kid on a bike!

Whirr! A ladybug lifts off a leaf and zooms into the bright blue sky.

Ladybugs are amazing flyers. They zip through the air on tiny wings. A ladybug can take off from a leaf in less than one second flat!

Once airborne, a ladybug can fly up to 30 miles in a single day. It can reach high into the sky — even above the clouds! Strong winds can carry them very far from home.

On the ground, ladybugs crawl on six tiny legs. They move slowly from leaf to leaf, exploring every stem along the way.

DAY LIFE

DID YOU KNOW?
On warm days, ladybugs spread their wings and sunbathe on leaves to warm up!

Chirp! The morning birds call, and a ladybug wakes to start its day.

Ladybugs are busy during the day. They wake up when the sun warms the air. Then they spend hours crawling and flying from plant to plant, hunting for food.

On hot days, ladybugs rest in the shade. They sit under leaves to cool down. When it rains, they hide under bark or squeeze into a small crack.

At night, ladybugs find a safe spot to sleep. They tuck under a leaf and stay perfectly still until morning comes again.

LOVELINESS

FUN FACT!
A group of ladybugs gathering for winter is called a 'loveliness' — the perfect name!

Rustle! Hundreds of ladybugs huddle together under a big log.

Most of the time, ladybugs live alone. They walk and hunt by themselves. But when winter comes, everything changes.

In the cold months, ladybugs come together in huge groups. Thousands of them may gather in one spot! They pile up under logs, rocks, or inside cracks in walls.

Staying close keeps them warm through the cold. A big group shares body heat to survive. When spring returns, they spread out and go their own way again.

LOVE BUGS

A female ladybug can lay up to 1,000 eggs in just one summer!

Tap! Two ladybugs meet on a stem and touch their feelers together.

In spring, ladybugs look for a mate. Males find females by following their special scent. Their antennae help them pick up the smell from far away.

When two ladybugs meet, they tap feelers. This is how they say hello! If they are a good match, they will mate.

After mating, the female looks for a safe place to lay her eggs. She picks a leaf that has plenty of aphids nearby. Her babies will need food the moment they hatch.

LITTLE LARVAE

Crack! A strange looking insect crawls on a leaf.

Baby ladybugs do not look like their parents at all. They are called **larvae**. A larva is long and dark with tiny spikes on its back. It looks more like a tiny dinosaur than a ladybug!

Larvae start eating right away. They munch on aphids and grow fast. As they grow, they shed their skin several times. This is called molting.

After a few weeks, the larva sticks to a leaf and forms a hard shell called a **pupa**. Inside, its body changes completely into an adult ladybug.

GROW UP

A new adult ladybug gets its spots in just a few hours after coming out!

Pop! A brand new ladybug starts to push out of its pupa shell at last.

Mother ladybugs do not stay with their eggs. They lay them and fly away. The babies must take care of themselves from the very start.

When a new ladybug comes out of its pupa, it is soft and pale. Its shell has no color yet! Over the next few hours, it gets harder and turns bright red or orange.

The young ladybug is now on its own. It must find food and stay safe from predators. In about one year, it will be ready to have babies of its own.

SUPER SUCCESS

Hum! A ladybug lands on a garden plant and gets right to work.

Ladybugs are a big help to people. They eat pests that damage plants and crops. Farmers and gardeners are always glad to have them around!

But some ladybugs are in trouble. Habitat loss and bug sprays can hurt them. When fields are sprayed, ladybugs lose their food and homes.

We can help ladybugs by planting flowers and keeping bug sprays away. A healthy garden is a great home for these helpful insects. Every ladybug we protect helps our gardens grow.

SPOT SOME

If a ladybug lands on you, try counting its spots before it flies away!

Psst! A ladybug sits very still on a bright garden flower.

You can find ladybugs in your own yard! Look on plants with tiny bugs, like roses or bean plants. Ladybugs always go where the food is.

Spring and summer are the best times to look. Check sunny spots on warm days. Look under leaves and along stems for these tiny visitors hiding in plain sight.

If you find one, watch it closely but be gentle. You can let it walk on your hand. Then place it back on a leaf when you are done. Happy ladybug hunting!

GLOSSARY

aphids

Tiny soft bugs that live on plants and suck their juice

antennae

Thin feelers on an insect's head used to smell and touch

larvae

Baby insects that look very different from the adults

pupa

A hard case where a larva changes into an adult insect

elytra

The hard wing covers that protect a ladybug's soft wings